FOCUS ON
Comprehension
2

Louis Fidge

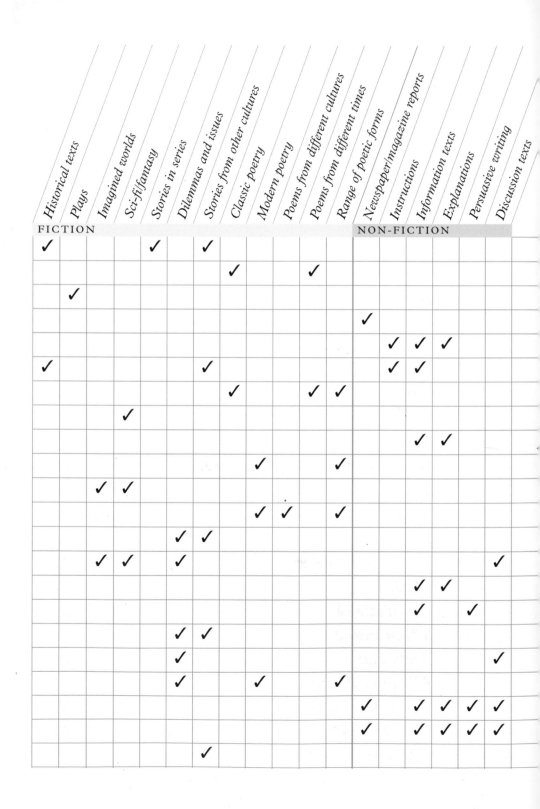

FICTION												NON-FICTION					
Historical texts	Plays	Imagined worlds	Sci-fi/fantasy	Stories in series	Dilemmas and issues	Stories from other cultures	Classic poetry	Modern poetry	Poems from different cultures	Poems from different times	Range of poetic forms	Newspaper/magazine reports	Instructions	Information texts	Explanations	Persuasive writing	Discussion texts
✓				✓		✓											
							✓			✓							
	✓																
												✓					
													✓	✓	✓		
✓						✓							✓	✓			
							✓		✓	✓							
		✓															
														✓	✓		
								✓		✓							
	✓	✓															
							✓	✓		✓							
				✓	✓												
	✓	✓	✓													✓	
														✓	✓		
				✓	✓												
				✓													✓
				✓				✓		✓							
												✓		✓	✓	✓	✓
												✓		✓	✓	✓	✓
					✓												

Contents

UNIT 1   The House on the Prairie

Think ahead

Look at the picture. Is the story set in modern times?

Men were busily working on new buildings down Main
Street. Shavings and sawdust and ends of boards were
scattered on the muddy and trampled young grass in the
street, and wheels had cut deep ruts through it. Through
the frames of buildings that did not have sidings on yet,
and down alleys between the buildings, and beyond both
ends of the street, the clean, green prairie rippled far away
and quiet under the clear sky, but the town was troubled
and noisy with rasping saws and pounding hammers and
the thud of boxes and sharp crash of boards unloaded from
wagons, and men talking loudly.

Timidly Laura and Carrie waited to let Pa's wagon
come up, and they led Mary along beside it until they
came to the corner where Pa's building was.

The tall false fronts loomed up, cutting off half the sky.
Pa's building had a front door, with a glass window at

each side. The door opened into one long room. Far at
its other side was a back door, and near it a side window.
The floor was wide boards, and the walls were boards
with daylight coming through the cracks and knotholes.
That was all.

From *By the Shores of the Silver Lake* by Laura Ingalls Wilder

➡ *Thinking back*

Answer these questions in proper sentences.
1 What was Pa travelling in?
2 Who was waiting for Pa's wagon?
3 What was the new house made of?
4 How many rooms were there in the new house?

➡ *Thinking about it*

1 List some sounds you might hear in the town.
2 How can you tell the town is new?
3 What is all round the town?
4 What time of year do you think it was? Say why.

➡ *Thinking it through*

1 What clues are there in the passage and in the
  picture that the story took place some time ago?
2 Where do you think Laura and her family have
  come from? Why do you think they have chosen to
  build a house where they have?
3 Write about some of the problems you think the
  family might have in the future.
4 Write about some of the things you would miss most
  if you had to move to a new town.

UNIT 2 Waiting

Think ahead

Time always seems to go slowly when you are waiting for something special! What special occasions always seem to take a long time arriving?

Waiting, waiting, waiting,
For the party to begin;
Waiting, waiting, waiting
For the laughter and din;
Waiting, waiting, waiting
With hair just so
And clothes trim and tidy
From top-knot to toe.
The floor is all shiny,
The lights are ablaze;
There are sweetmeats in plenty
And cakes beyond praise.
Oh the games and dancing,
The tricks and toys
The music and the madness
The colour and noise!
Waiting, waiting, waiting
For the first knock on the door –
Was ever such waiting,
Such waiting before?

From *Waiting* by James Reeves

> *Thinking back*

Choose the correct word from the brackets to complete each sentence.
1 The poet is waiting for the (match, party, film) to begin.
2 The poet's (clothes, books, toys) are trim and tidy.
3 The (door, table, floor) is all shiny.
4 The (lights, fires, candles) are ablaze.
5 There are plenty of (sandwiches, jellies, sweetmeats).

> *Thinking about it*

1 How can you tell the poet:
   a) has just brushed his or her hair?
   b) has his or her best clothes on?
2 What has made the 'floor all shiny'?
3 What food is mentioned in the poem?
4 List five things the poet is looking forward to.
5 Do you think it is a party for grown-ups or children? Explain your answer.

> *Thinking it through*

1 How can you tell the poet is very excited?
2 How many times does the poet repeat the line 'Waiting, waiting, waiting'? Why do you think this is?
3 Why do you think the poem ends with, 'Was ever such waiting, Such waiting before?'
4 The poem was written some time ago. What words in the poem give you a clue?
5 What sort of things do you do when you are waiting for something special to happen?

UNIT 3   When Dad Came Home

Think ahead

How can you tell this passage is taken from a playscript?

LILY ROSE Here's Dad coming now. Hello Dad, we're just talking about you.

MR RUGGLES Hello all. Well don't just talk about me, Lily Rose. What about my tea?

LILY ROSE Mum says I can't have any jam for my tea today because I burnt the clothes.

JOHN What did you burn, Lily Rose?

JAMES I hope you haven't burnt my new football shorts.

MRS RUGGLES Our precious Lily Rose got let out early from school and came home and burnt my ironing blanket and a good silk petticoat too.

LILY ROSE I was only trying to help. I wanted to give Mum a lovely surprise when she got home with the little ones. I wanted her to come in and find that great pile of ironing done.

MR RUGGLES It's no good crying over spilt milk, that's what I say.

JOHN Did she spill the milk, Dad?

JAMES No, Lily Rose didn't spill the milk. She burnt the clothes.

MR RUGGLES We know she didn't spill the milk out of the jug, boys. It's just a saying. It means it's no good getting upset about things going wrong after they've happened.

From *The Family from One End Street* adapted by Sheila Lane and Marion Kemp

► Thinking back

The beginnings and endings of these sentences have got mixed up. Write each sentence out correctly.

1 Mr and Mrs Ruggles   his tea.
2 Lily Rose was let out   are the mother and father of the family.

3 Lily Rose was trying   of school early.
4 Mr Ruggles wanted   to help her Mum.

► Thinking about it

1 Is Dad home at the start of the play?
  How can you tell?
2 Where do you think this play takes place?
  Give your reasons.
3 Is Lily Rose older than her brothers John and James?
  How can you tell?
4 What does 'it's no use crying over spilt milk' mean?

► Thinking it through

1 Read all the things Mrs Ruggles says again.
  What can you learn about her from these lines?
2 Why are playscripts set out like the one opposite?
  How does this help actors?
3 Write a sentence explaining what a narrator is.
  (Use a dictionary if you are not sure.)
4 Continue the story. Make up a few more lines of the playscript.

UNIT 4 Workman hurt in Explosion

Think ahead
How important are headlines in newspapers?
What do you expect this article to be about?

WORKMAN HURT IN EXPLOSION

A workman was seriously injured when a gas cylinder exploded on a demolition site on Tuesday. A JCB digger struck a gas cylinder at Farr's Factory in Oakley Road, Bedford. Builders were demolishing an old disused building at the time.

The explosion blew a door off its hinges and knocked a wall down. The driver of the digger, Tim O'Donovan, aged 30, was struck by flying debris and taken to the local hospital. The digger was severely damaged.

A local resident heard the explosion and called the fire service just after 1.30 pm. Firefighters were soon on the scene and gave first aid until an ambulance arrived. Station Officer Adrian Townsend said, 'We had a report from a neighbour who heard a very loud bang and then saw clouds of dust going up. When the

Scene of accident

crew got to the incident there we found that the front cab of the JCB was completely destroyed and the driver trapped inside. We had to cut him out.'

Mr O'Donovan received bad wounds in his stomach and groin. His condition was described by a doctor as 'comfortable' when we telephoned the hospital earlier today.

Thinking back

Answer these questions with proper sentences.
1 What caused the explosion?
2 Who was injured?
3 Where did the accident happen?
4 Who reported the explosion?
5 Who got to the scene first?
6 What wounds did Mr O'Donovan receive?

Thinking about it

Re-write these sentences in the correct order so they tell what happened.
• The gas cylinder exploded.
• The fire fighters arrived and rescued Mr O'Donovan.
• Mr O'Donovan was demolishing an old building.
• Mr O'Donovan was taken to hospital.
• He struck a gas cylinder.
• A local resident telephoned for help.

Thinking it through

1 Do you think this is a story or did it really happen? Explain your answer.
2 Why do you think headlines are usually written in capital letters?
3 If you were a police officer investigating the accident, what questions would you want to ask
   a) the owners of the factory?   b) the driver?
   c) the local resident who reported the accident?
4 Write an account of the accident from Mr O'Donovan's point of view.

UNIT 5 Playing Three-Hole

Think ahead

What games do you like playing? Three-Hole is a simple game that is easy to play outside.

WHAT IS THREE-HOLE?
Three-Hole is a game of marbles for two players. Children in Guyana enjoy playing this game.

WHAT DO YOU NEED?
Each player has three marbles.
You need to make three holes in the ground or sand with your finger or a stick, big enough for the marbles to go in. The holes should be a little distance apart.

WHAT ARE THE RULES OF THREE-HOLE?
- The game is played by taking it in turns to roll or flick the marbles.
- The idea is to try to get each marble into one of the holes.
- If a marble does not go into a hole the first time, at the next turn it can be rolled again from the point where it landed.
- Players can try to knock their opponent's marbles out of the way, rather than try to get their marble in a hole if they wish.
- The winner is the first to get their three marbles in the holes.

Choose a suitable word to fill in each gap.
1 Three-Hole is a game for _____ players.
2 The children in _____ play Three-Hole a lot.
3 Each player needs some _____ to play.
4 You need to make three _____ in the ground.

▶ *Thinking about it*

1 Why is Three-Hole an outside game?
2 Is it true that you don't need a lot of equipment to play the game?
3 What can you tell about the weather in Guyana from the passage and the picture?
4 How is the game won?

▶ *Thinking it through*

1 The text is set out under three headings.
   Why is this helpful?
2 What would be the best way to check that the information in the text is clear and accurate?
3 Why do games need to have rules?
4 What do you think of children who cheat at games or who break the rules?

UNIT 6 A Viking Raid

Think ahead

What sort of things does your school write to your parents about?

Dear Parents

A VIKING RAID

As part of the Norsetional Curriculum, we are required to develop the educational experiences of Viking warriors. Your son has the opportunity to develop his fighting skills on our Viking raid to the Baltic Sea. There will be plenty of opportunities for educational plunder and slaughter, and it is hoped that your son will join in all such activities. It must be stressed that bad behaviour on such trips is important for the good name of the Vikings. If your son is not violent enough, he will be sent home and not allowed on any more raids. He will also be thought of as a bit of a softy.

Depart: Dawn, from the jetty at Oslofyord
Return: For those still alive after the raid, we hope to arrive back home in about half a year.

Things to take
Chain mail
Iron helmet (if you can afford one)
Leather tunic
Boots (proper Viking boots, no plimsolls please!)
Cloak
Mittens or gloves
Spare trousers (in case you get blood on the ones you're wearing)

Chest to put all the above in (and to sit on in the ship whilst rowing)
Axe
Knife
Ash wood spear
Double-edged sword
Large round shield
Bow and arrows
Cooking utensils
Water

Lunchbox (dried or smoked fish, smoked walrus meat, cheese, bread)
Comb (to look neat and tidy)
Pocket money (although there will be an opportunity to seize money, slaves and souvenirs from the places we raid)

Yours sincerely
Erik Bloodaxe

PS. No girls allowed. They must stay at home and look after the farms whilst the men are away.

From *The Lost Diary of Eric Bloodaxe* by Steve Barlow and Steve Skidmore

➡ Thinking back

Choose the correct answer for each question.
1 The letter is about
   a) a Viking ship b) a Viking soldier c) a Viking raid
2 It is from
   a) Eric Bluesword b) Eric Bloodaxe c) Eric Bluebottle
3 The letter is to
   a) children b) parents c) teachers
4 The trip is to
   a) The Baltic Sea b) Britain c) Norway
5 The trip will take about
   a) a year b) six months c) a month

➡ Thinking about it

1 What is the purpose of the trip?
2 Why do you think bad behaviour is required?
3 What items of clothing are listed?
4 What weapons are to be taken?
5 Who do you think Eric Bloodaxe might be?

➡ Thinking it through

1 Do you think this is intended to be a serious or a
   humorous letter? Why?
2 How can you tell it was supposed to have been
   written some time ago?
3 We can learn a lot about the Vikings from this letter.
   Write and say what you have discovered about:
   a) their clothes b) weapons c) diet d) life-style (were
   they farmers, for instance?) e) differences in way
   men and women were treated.

UNIT 7 From a Railway Carriage

Think ahead
How can you tell this poem is about an old-fashioned train?

Faster than fairies, faster than witches,
Bridges and houses, hedges and ditches;
And charging along like troops in a battle,
All through the meadows the horses and cattle:
All of the sights of the hill and the plain
Fly as thick as driving rain;
And ever again, in the wink of an eye,
Painted stations whistle by.

Here is a child who clambers and scrambles,
All by himself and gathering brambles;
Here is a tramp who stands and gazes;
And there is the green for stringing the daisies!
Here is a cart away in the road
Lumping along with man and load;
And here is a mill, and there is a river:
Each a glimpse and gone for ever!

From *A Child's Garden of Verses* by Robert Louis Stevenson

➤ *Thinking back*

Think of a suitable word to fill in each gap.

1 The train goes faster than _____ .
2 The train passes through _____ .
3 Painted _____ whistle by.
4 The child is gathering _____ .
5 A _____ stands and gazes at the train.
6 On the road there is a man in a _____ .

➤ *Thinking about it*

1 How can you tell the train is going fast?
2 What do you think 'in a wink of an eye' means?
3 List ten things that are seen from the train as it speeds along.
4 How can painted stations 'whistle' by?
5 What does 'each a glimpse and gone for ever' mean?
6 What noises do you think you would hear if you were on the train?

➤ *Thinking it through*

1 Is this a modern poem? Give your reasons.
2 a) How many verses are there in the poem?
   b) How many lines are there in each verse?
   c) Is it a rhyming poem?
   d) Write four pairs of rhyming words from the poem.
   e) What do you notice about the rhythm of the poem when you say it aloud?
3 What did you think of the poem? Give your reasons.
4 Who wrote the poem? See what you can find out about him.

UNIT 8   The Iron Man

Think ahead

Look at the picture. What sort of person or thing do you think the Iron Man is?

The Iron Man came to the top of the cliff.

How far had he walked? Nobody knows. Where had he come from? Nobody knows. How was he made? Nobody knows.

Taller than a house, the Iron Man stood at the top of the cliff, on the very brink, in the darkness.

The wind sang through his iron fingers. His great iron head, shaped like a dustbin but as big as a bedroom, slowly turned to the right, slowly turned to the left. His iron ears turned this way, that way. He was hearing the sea. His eyes, like headlamps, glowed white, then red, then infra-red, searching the sea. Never before had the Iron Man seen the sea.

He swayed in the strong wind that pressed against his back. He swayed forward, on the brink of the high cliff.

And his right foot, his enormous right foot, lifted – up, out, into space, and the Iron Man stepped forward, off the cliff, into nothingness.

CRRRAAAASSSSSSH!

From *The Iron Man* by Ted Hughes

Think of a suitable word to fill in each gap.
The Iron Man came to the __1__ of the cliff. Nobody knew where he had come __2__ . Nobody knew __3__ he was made. He was taller than a __4__ . His __5__ was shaped like a dustbin. His __6__ turned this way and that. The Iron Man could hear the __7__ . His eyes were like __8__ . His eyes changed colour. He had __9__ seen the sea before. There was a __10__ wind. It made the Iron Man sway. The Iron Man __11__ off the cliff. He __12__ down with a loud noise.

Thinking about it

1 Where did the events in this passage take place?
2 What was the weather like? How can you tell?
3 Why do you think the Iron Man had come?
4 Do you think the Iron Man is friendly or fierce? Give your reasons.
5 What do you think will happen next?

Thinking it through

1 Do you think this is an exciting start to a story? Why?
2 What do you think the author means when he says the wind 'sang' through the Iron Man's fingers'?
3 Why does the author write 'Crash' like this 'CRRRAAAASSSSSSH!'?
4 Does this passage make you want to read the rest of the story? Why?

UNIT 9 Bats

Think ahead
Some people are afraid of bats. Are you?

Some bat facts
There are nearly 1,000 types of
bats. They are very clean animals.
They don't like dusty places. Bats
do not damage buildings. They
are gentle, intelligent creatures.
They will not attack you.

What are bats?
Bats are flying mammals,
like small mice with wings.
They have furry bodies,
big ears and big eyes.

Where do bats live?
You can find bats all over the world. They usually live in
groups. Bats often live in caves or roost in trees. Some bats
make their homes in buildings.

What do bats eat?
Bats eat mainly insects and fruit. They often catch insects
while they are flying. Bats usually come out at night and
hunt in the dark.

Are bats blind?
Bats use their ears more than their eyes. They make high-
pitched squeaks which bounce off objects like echoes. By
listening to the echoes, bats can work out how near they
are to objects. Bats never bump into things!

Thinking back

Write a sentence to answer each question.
1 How many types of bats are there?
2 What do bats look like?
3 Where do bats live?
4 How do bats catch insects?
5 Which do bats use most – their ears or their eyes?

Thinking about it

1 How can you tell bats are clean animals?
2 Explain what a mammal is.
3 Why don't you see many bats during the day?
4 Why do bats give off high-pitched squeaks?

Thinking it through

1 Which of the facts about bats did you find most
  interesting? Why?
2 Why do you think some people are afraid of bats?
3 How could you check the facts given in the passage
  if you needed to?
4 Some people say that bats eat blood. What would
  you tell them?

UNIT 10   Don't Put Mustard in the Custard

Think ahead
Look at the title of the poem.
What sort of a poem do you think it is going to be?

Don't do,
Don't do,
Don't do that.
Don't pull faces.
Don't tease the cat

Don't pick your ears.
Don't be rude at school.
Who do they think I am?

Some kind of fool?

One day
they'll say
Don't put toffee in my
   coffee.
Don't pour gravy on the
   baby.
Don't put beer in his ear.
Don't stick your toes up
   his nose.

Don't put confetti in the
   spaghetti
and don't squash peas on
   your knees.

Don't put ants in your
   pants.
Don't put mustard in the
   custard.
Don't chuck jelly at the telly
and don't throw fruit at the
   computer.
Don't throw fruit at the
   computer.

Don't what?
Don't throw fruit at the
   computer.
Don't what?
Don't throw fruit at the
   computer.
Who do they think I am?
Some kind of fool?

From *Don't Put Mustard in the Custard* by Michael Rosen

Copy this list of rules and fill in the missing words.
1 Don't pull _____ .
2 Don't be rude at _____ .
3 Don't put toffee in my _____ .
4 Don't pour gravy on the _____ .
5 Don't put confetti in the _____ .
6 Don't squash peas on your _____ .

→ *Thinking about it*

1 Do you think the poem is supposed to be written by an adult or a child? Say why you give your answer.
2 Who do you think is giving all the rules?
3 What does the writer mean when he says, 'What do they think I am? Some kind of fool?'
4 What makes you think that the writer of the poem is fed up with being given orders?

→ *Thinking it through*

1 What did you think of the poem? Give your opinion.
2 What is the difference between the first few rules and the rules that come after 'One day they'll say ...'? Are the rules all sensible?
3 Would you say that this is just a nonsense poem or is the writer also trying to make a point? Explain your answer.
4 Notice how the writer uses rhyming in some lines such as 'Don't put <u>ants</u> in your <u>pants</u>.' Make up a few more rules and use rhyming words in the same way.

UNIT 11　The Cowardly Lion

Think ahead

What are lions usually like?
Is it unusual to find a 'cowardly' lion? Why?

The King of Beasts shouldn't be a coward,' said the Scarecrow.

'I know it,' returned the Lion, wiping a tear from his eye with the tip of his tail; 'it is my great sorrow, and makes my life very unhappy. But whenever there is danger my heart begins to beat fast.'

'Perhaps you have heart disease,' said the Tin Woodman.

'It may be,' said the Lion.

'If you have,' continued the Tin Woodman,' you ought to be glad, for it proves you have a heart. For my part, I have no heart; so I cannot have heart disease.'

'Perhaps,' said the Lion, thoughtfully, 'if I had no heart I should not be a coward.'

'Have you brains?' asked the Scarecrow.

'I suppose so. I've never looked to see,' replied the Lion.

'I am going to the great Oz to ask him to give me some,' remarked the Scarecrow, 'for my head is stuffed with straw.'

'And I am going to ask him to give me a heart,' said the Woodman.

'Do you think Oz could give me courage?' asked the Cowardly Lion.

From *The Wizard of Oz* by L Frank Baum

Thinking back

Which character said each of the following things:
1 'The King of Beasts shouldn't be a coward.'
2 'Perhaps you have heart disease.'
3 'My head is stuffed with straw.'
4 'Do you think Oz could give me courage?'

Thinking about it

1 The Lion, the Tin Woodman and the Scarecrow each have a problem. Say what is the matter with each one.
2 Who does each character hope will help them solve their problems?
3 How can you tell that being a coward makes the Lion unhappy?
4 What happens whenever the Lion is in danger?

Thinking it through

1 What sort of a man is the Great Oz? (Look at the title of the book!)
2 Why do you think all the characters hope he will be able to help them?
3 Make up your own definition of the word 'coward'.
4 Is there anything you are really frightened of? Does that make you a coward? Explain your answer.

I love the ...

What are your favourite smells – fresh bread?
newly cut grass? the sea? something else?

I love the ...

friday night
smell of
mammie baking
bread – creeping
up to me in
bed, and tho
zzzz I'll fall
asleep, before i
even get a
bite – when
morning come,
you can bet
I'll meet a
kitchen table
laden with
bread, still
warm and fresh
salt bread
sweet bread
crisp and brown
& best of all
coconut buns
THAT's why
I love the
friday night
smell of mammie
baking bread
putting me to
sleep, dreaming
of jumping from
the highest branch
of the jamoon tree
into the red water
creek
beating calton
run & catching
the biggest fish
in the world
plus, getting
the answers right
to every single
sum
that every day
in my dream
begins and ends
with the friday
night smell of
mammie baking
bread, and
coconut buns
of course

From *A Caribbean Dozen* by Marc Matthews

Thinking back

1 When does the poet's Mum do her baking?
2 Where is the poet when he smells the baking?
3 What sort of tree does he dream he is jumping?
4 Who does he dream he beats?
5 What sort of fish does he dream he catches?

Thinking about it

1 What does the 'zzzz' in the poem mean?
2 What does the poet mean when he says
   a) 'I'll meet a kitchen table laden with bread'?
   b) the smell 'puts him to sleep'?
3 Why is Friday night special?

Thinking it through

1 What sort of pictures do you get in your mind when you read this poem?
2 Did you enjoy the poem? Give your reasons.
3 What do you notice about the language of the poem? Which country do you think it comes from?
4 In what ways does the poem not follow the rules of grammar and punctuation?

UNIT 13 Amazing Grace

Think ahead

Read the introductory paragraph. How do you think Nana (Grace's grandmother) can help Grace?

Grace was unhappy. Some children said she couldn't be Peter Pan in the school play because she was black and Peter Pan was a boy. Her Nana said that Grace could be anything she wanted if she put her mind to it. Nana decided to take Grace to see a ballet, Romeo and Juliet.

Nana showed Grace some pictures of a beautiful young girl dancer in a tutu. 'STUNNING NEW JULIET' it said on one of them.

'That one is little Rosalie from back home in Trinidad,' said Nana. 'Her granny and me, we grew up together on the island. She's always asking me do I want tickets to see her little girl dance – so this time I said yes.'

After the ballet Grace played the part of Juliet, dancing around her room in her imaginary tutu. 'I can do anything I want,' she thought. 'I can even be Peter Pan.'

On Monday they had the auditions. Their teacher let the class vote on the parts. Raj was chosen to play Captain Hook. Natalie was going to be Wendy. Then they had to choose Peter Pan. Grace knew exactly what to do and all the words she had to say. It was the part she had often played at home. All the children voted for her. 'You were great,' said Natalie.

From *Amazing Grace* by Mary Hoffman and Caroline Binch

Thinking back

Think of a suitable ending for each sentence.
1 Grace was unhappy because _____ .
2 Nana told Grace that she could _____ .
3 Nana took Grace to _____ .
4 In the ballet, the part of Juliet was played by _____ .
5 After the ballet Grace _____ .
6 All the children voted for _____ .

Thinking about it

Answer these questions with proper sentences in your book.
1 In what way were some children unkind to Grace at school?
2 What do you think Nana meant when she said that Grace 'could be anything she wanted if she put her mind to it'?
3 How did going to the ballet help Grace?

Thinking it through

Answer these questions with proper sentences in your book.
1 Did you feel sorry for Grace at the beginning? Why?
2 Grace was a determined girl. Is this true or false? Explain why.
3 What sort of person was Grace's Nana? Give reasons for your answer.
4 What do the following words mean? Use a dictionary if you are unsure.
   a) audition   b) tutu   c) ballet

UNIT 14   The Get-away Hen

Think ahead

Do you know what factory farming is?
Do you know what a battery hen is?

Brown Hen lived in a cage house full of hens. She sat in dim light and warm air, and soft music played, but she never saw night or the light of stars. All she could see was the roof of the house, which was painted a dull shade of yellow. She was fed by a machine tipping her food out into a tray. She could eat without stretching her neck.

'Thanks very much!' thought Brown Hen (though she didn't know who to thank). She pecked the food up, and then laid an egg. The egg rolled away down a chute, and she never saw it again.

Brown Hen was bored and she started complaining. 'Is this it?' she asked. 'Is this all there is to my life?'

'Maybe it is,' said the others. 'But you're well fed and warm, so shut up!'

'I want to find out what my life is about!' said Brown Hen, and she sat in her cage and dreamed of *something*. She didn't quite know what it was.

Then one night things went wrong. Someone pulled a switch by mistake and … the lights flickered out and the warm air turned cold. The soft music stopped and the doors of the cages popped wide open.

From *The Get-away Hen* by **Martin Waddell**

Thinking back

Choose the correct answer to finish each sentence.
1 Brown Hen never saw
   a) other hens b) the stars c) the roof of her house
2 A machine tipped food
   a) into a tray b) into her mouth c) into her cage
3 When Brown Hen laid an egg it rolled away
   a) into a box b) through the bars c) down a chute
4 Brown Hen got
   a) sleepy b) hungry c) bored
5 One night the door of her cage
   a) popped wide open b) got stuck c) slammed shut

Thinking about it

1 What were the advantages and disadvantages of living in the cage house?
2 Why did Brown Hen get fed up?
3 Why did the other hens tell her to shut up?
4 What did the switch control?

Thinking it through

1 In what ways do you think the farmer was kind?
2 In what ways was the farmer being unfair?
3 How do you think Brown Hen felt when her cage door popped open?
4 Write some sentences and say how you think the story might continue.

UNIT 15   Whales

Perhaps the most amazing thing about the whale is not its size but the fact that it is a mammal and not a fish. Since the whale is a mammal, the baby whale is fed on its mother's milk. Baby whales are not hatched from eggs but are born alive.

Whales have no gills and breathe air through their lungs. When a whale needs to breathe it comes to the surface. Whales breathe through a hole on the top of their heads called a blow hole. Underneath the water these holes are closed by little valves. Whales can remain under the water for 45 minutes or so.

Whales are warm-blooded animals. They have a thick layer of 'blubber' (like fat) under the skin to help keep them warm.

Whales feed on smaller sea creatures and use sounds to 'talk' to each other. They have fins and strong tails to help them swim. Whales usually swim together in groups. These groups are called schools of whales. There are over 30 different sorts of whales.

FASCINATING FACTS
*The largest whale in existence today is the blue whale.
It can grow up to 30 metres long. About one third of
the length of the animal is taken up by its head!*

Think of a sensible ending for each sentence.
1 A whale is not a fish. It is a _____ .
2 Baby whales are not hatched from eggs but are born
 _____ .

3 When a whale needs to breathe it _____ .
4 Under their skins whales have a thick layer of
 _____ .

5 To help them swim, whales have _____ .
6 A group of whales is called a _____ .

▶ *Thinking about it*

Answer these questions in your book.
1 Explain what a whale uses a 'blow hole' for.
2 Why do you think they have little valves on their
 blow holes?
3 Why do you think blubber is important to whales?
4 Which type of whale is the largest living animal?
5 Do whales normally travel about on their own or in
 groups?
6 Why do you think whales prefer to be in groups?

▶ *Thinking it through*

Answer these questions in your book.
1 Whales are mammals. What does this mean?
2 Whales use 'sounds' to 'talk' to each other. What do
 you think this means?
3 Why can't whales just swim under water all the time?
4 Name three other large sea animals that you can
 think of.

UNIT 16 Advertisements

Think ahead

What is your favourite advertisement? Why?

We see advertisements every day. Most of them are trying to sell us something. Look at some of the ways advertisers try to persuade us to buy their product.

Thinking back

Write answers to these questions.
1 What is the purpose of advertisements?
2 What is this advertisement trying to sell?
3 How does the advertisment describe the graphics?
4 What is the jingle (the rhyme) that the
   advertisement uses?
5 Why is the person telling you to hurry to get the game?

Thinking about it

1 What do you think of the name of the game? Why?
2 How can you tell the game has just come out?
3 What does 'sensational' mean?
4 List some of the claims the advertiser makes about
   their product. Do you think they are true?
5 In what way do you think the picture might help
   persuade you to buy the game?

Thinking it through

1 Why do you think the advertisers
   a) use capital letters in places?
   b) make some words bigger than others?
   c) use colour in the way they do?
2 Do the advertisers use long sentences to tell you
   about Racing Rockets? Why not?
3 Why do you think a jingle is used?
4 How successful is this advert? Say what you like, or
   don't like about it.

UNIT 17 A New Friend

Think ahead
What is it like to be lonely?

'I'll be your friend, if you want,' said Ian, 'I don't have any friends either.' Elizabeth looked back at the classroom.

'They laugh at me too,' said Ian, 'because of these.' He pointed to each of his eyes in turn and Elizabeth noticed that one was brown and the other blue.

'Oh,' said Elizabeth. Ian Fuller made a rude sign with his fingers and Elizabeth copied.

'Elizabeth John Baptiste!' said Mrs Gregg, catching Elizabeth in the act.

'I didn't do noffin,' Elizabeth pleaded.

Elizabeth went to sit down next to Ian Fuller, who slumped across his desk and stared out of the window. She did not really mind his eyes, in fact they were quite special.

She'd never seen anybody with anything quite so special before. Miss Gregg did not ask Elizabeth any more questions but every so often she smiled at her to show she had not forgotten that she was there. When the bell rang everybody ran outside. Elizabeth did not know where to go.

'You coming?' Ian called from the doorway. Elizabeth followed him, pretending she did not want to go.

From *Mammy, Sugar Falling Down* by Trish Cooke

➤ *Thinking back*

Match up the beginnings and endings of these sentences correctly.

1 Ian wanted to be   Ian out to play.
2 The children laughed   everybody ran outside.
   at Ian because
3 Elizabeth sat next to   Elizabeth's friend.
4 When the bell went   Ian Fuller in class.
5 Elizabeth followed   his eyes were different
                         colours.

➤ *Thinking about it*

Answer these questions in your book.

1 Why didn't Ian have any friends?
2 Why did Ian make a rude sign at Elizabeth?
3 Who was Mrs Gregg?
4 How can you tell Mrs Gregg is surprised at Elizabeth's behaviour?
5 How can you tell Mrs Gregg is a nice teacher?

➤ *Thinking it through*

Answer these questions in your book.

1 How did the other children tease Ian?
2 Did Elizabeth mind Ian's eyes? How can you tell?
3 Which of the adjectives below could be used to describe Ian?
   kind   thoughtful   rude   lonely   unfriendly
4 In what ways could you make a new boy or girl feel welcomed and accepted in your class. What sort of things would you do?

UNIT 18 Fair's Fair

Think ahead

What would it be like to be homeless and hungry in the middle of winter? What sort of problems would you face?

Huge, as big as a donkey, nearly, with eyes like street lamps and jaws like an oven door. Down the street it padded, with a glare to the right and a glare to the left, and a savage twitch of its great black nose. Somebody opened a window and threw a bucket of dirty water down; and the black dog snarled with rage. Up it came to the doorstep where Jackson sat and steamed. It glared and growled while the snowflakes fried on its nose.

'Shove off!' wailed Jackson, hiding his pie and shaking in his shoes – or, rather, in his feet as he had no shoes worth mentioning. 'I got no food and I'm only skin and bone myself so I'll taste as sour as leaves.'

'Liar!' said the dog; not in words but with its terrible eyes and rattling teeth.

'I'm froze and hungry!' wailed Jackson, wishing he'd eaten the pie.

'And I'm froze and hungry!' said the dog not in words but with its lean sides and smoking breath.

'All right,' said Jackson, seeing there was no help for it. 'Fair's fair. Half for you and half for me.' And he broke the pie and the dog swallowed down half with a fearful guzzle and growl. 'Fair's fair,' said Jackson, and ate what's left. 'Now shove off!'

From *Fair's Fair* by Leon Garfield

Think of a suitable word to fill each gap.
The dog was nearly as big as a __1__ . It had __2__ like street lamps and __3__ like an oven door. When somebody __4__ a bucket of water over it, the dog __5__ with rage. Jackson __6__ his pie and __7__ the dog to go away. __8__ said he was frozen and __9__ . The dog would not go away, so Jackson gave it __10__ of his pie.

Thinking about it

1 What was the weather like?
2 How can you tell the dog was not well fed?
3 How did Jackson feel when he saw the dog?
4 Where do you think Jackson was?
5 How can you tell Jackson is poor?
6 How can you tell Jackson is not well educated by the way he talks?

Thinking it through

1 What do you think the author meant by 'eyes like street lamps and jaws like an oven door'?
2 The author uses lots of words, like glare, that show the dog to be frightening and fierce. Find and write five fierce words from the passage into your book.
3 The author says that 'snowflakes fried on the dog's nose'. What do you think he meant by this?
4 How did the dog 'talk' to Jackson?
5 Would you have given half your pie to the dog if you were starving? Why do you think Jackson did it?

UNIT 19 A Page of Poems

Think ahead

*Which of the poems below could also be called
'My Worst Week'?*

Four o'clock Friday

Four o'clock Friday, I'm home
at last.
Time to forget the week that
has passed.
On Monday, at break, they
stole my ball
And threw it over the playground wall.
On Tuesday morning, I came in late,
But they were waiting behind the gate.
On Wednesday afternoon, in games
They threw mud at me and called me names.
Yesterday, they laughed after the test
'Cause my marks were lower than the rest.
Today, they trampled my books on the floor
And I was kept in, because I swore.
Four o'clock, Friday, at last I'm free.
For two whole days they can't get at me.

From *Poems about Feelings* by John Foster

A-Z of food

A is for apples, lovely to crunch,
B is for bananas in a bunch.
C is for cake with candles alight
D is for doughnuts, soft to bite.

A Riddle

Hold it steady in
  your hand,
Then you will see
  another land,
Where right is left,
  and left is right,
And no sound stirs
  by day or night;
When you look in,
  yourself you see,
Yet in that place you
  cannot be.

Rain

Raindrops falling with a splash,
Angry black clouds argue and clash.
In town people run for cover.
No-one's sorry when it's all over!

Thinking back

Answer each question with true (T) or false (F).

1 *Four o'clock on Friday* is about making new friends.
2 A riddle is a kind of puzzle.
3 The *A-Z of Food* is in alphabetical order.
4 One of the poems is about a foggy day.
5 All the poems rhyme.

Thinking about it

1 a) On what day was *Four o'clock Friday* written?
  b) Where did most of the events take place in it?
  c) Why do you think the poet gets picked on?
2 Can you guess the answer to the riddle?
3 Think of some food beginning with E, F, G and H.
4 What does 'angry black clouds argue' mean?

Thinking it through

1 a) How does the poet make you feel sorry for him or
  her in *Four o'clock Friday*?
  b) If you saw a child being bullied what could you
  do to help?
2 Make up a riddle for a) a chair b) a towel
  c) a bed. (Your riddles do not have to rhyme!)
3 Make up a short acrostic poem for FOG. Set it out
  like the *Rain* poem.
4 Make up four more lines for the *A-Z of Food* poem.

UNIT 20   Who Cares Anyway?

Think ahead
What do you think this passage is going to be about?

A refugee is someone who has been forced to leave their own country. It is often because of war or famine.

My name is Nebiyou Assefa. I am 13, no, 14 – well, who cares anyway? I lived in Addis Abbaba in Ethiopia with my mother. In Addis I lived in a house in with toys and such happy things. When my mother died, my father said, 'Now you will live with me.'

I was happy just to play and be with my father. Then one day he went to a fighting place. From that time he didn't come back. Nobody cared. Everything was messy, cars were driving everywhere. People were afraid of one another, and nobody wanted to look after me.

The soldiers said they had to go to Kenya to refugee camps. Of course, I didn't know how to get to Kenya, I didn't even know what direction it was in.

Some soldiers took me to Kenya in a big car. I wanted to live with them in a refugee camp, but I am just a little boy and they said I had to live in the orphanage camp with the other orphan children.

We were sent to a camp called Kakuma. We have no family, so what are we going to do? I feel simply left here.

From *One Day We Had to Run* by Sybella Wilkes

Thinking back

Write these sentences in the correct order to tell Nebiyou's story.

a) Nebiyou's father went to fight but did not return.
b) Nebiyou was sent to a refugee camp called Kakuma.
c) Nebiyou lived with his mother when he was small.
d) Some soldiers took Nebiyou to Kenya in a big car.
e) When his mother died, he went to live with his father.

Thinking about it

1 Why doesn't Nebiyou know his exact birthday?
2 How do you know Nebiyou's mother and father did not live together?
3 What job did Nebiyou's father do?
4 How do you know there was a war?
5 Why do you think Nebiyou says 'nobody cared'?
6 Why did Nebiyou decide to go to Kenya?

Thinking it through

1 Do you think this is a true or a made-up story? Give your reasons.
2 How can you tell by the things Nebiyou says, that there was a feeling of panic everywhere at this time?
3 What do these words mean?
   a) orphan   b) orphanage   c) refugee
4 Write about some of the feelings and thoughts you had when you read Nebiyou's story.

UNIT 21 Daily Life in the Kakuma Refugee Camp

Think ahead

*Look back at Unit 20. What is a refugee?
What do you think a refugee camp is?*

At one time there were around 25,000 children in Kakuma Refugee Camp in Kenya, many of whom were orphans. They were well cared for and educated.

Washing – a job everyone hates! ▶

▲ Making bricks out of mud to build a house or school.

◀ Every day the boys take turns to queue up for water. Another job everyone hates.

◀ The boys cook in groups of six. They are given wheat flour, cabbage, oil and sugar.

◀ Having fun! Many refugees are quite used to seeing journalists and photographers in the camp and are not scared to show off!

Grinding wheat to make chapatis, a kind of flat bread. ▶

**From *One Day We Had to Run*
by Sybella Wilkes**

44

▶ Thinking back

Answer these questions with true (T) or false (F).
1 The name of the camp is the Kenya Refugee Camp.
2 The two jobs everyone hates are washing and queuing up for water.
3 Chapatis are made from ground rice.
4 A chapati is something you wear.
5 Bricks can be made of mud.
6 The boys are not allowed to cook.

▶ Thinking about it

1 What is the weather like in Kenya? How can you tell?
2 Why do you think everyone hates getting water?
3 Do you think the children are happy most of the time? Give reasons for your answer.
4 Describe how mud bricks are made.
5 List some of ways the lives of the refugee children are different from the things you are used to.

▶ Thinking it through

1 What do you think you would you find difficult about living in a refugee camp?
2 What do you think you would enjoy about the life in a refugee camp?
3 What impression is the photographer trying to create with the 'photographs'? Explain your answer.
4 Imagine you are a refugee in the camp. Write an account of what you think an ordinary day in your life would be like.

UNIT 22 Grandpa Chatterji

Think ahead

Have you ever had a visit from a relative you have never seen before? Did they turn out as you expected?

They waited and waited. Suddenly Sanjay shouted, 'They're here!' The little red Mini had pulled up outside the house.

'Oh dear,' cried Neetu, suddenly going all shy, 'I'm going to hide.'

They both hid behind the sofa. They heard the front door open. They heard Mum come in and say gently, 'Welcome to our home!' They heard Dad say, 'I'll take your luggage up to your room,' and they heard a thin, quiet, soft voice say, 'And where are my little grandchildren?'

Then there was silence. Crouched behind the sofa, Neetu and Sanjay hardly breathed. Then suddenly, although they didn't hear Grandpa Chatterji come into the room, they knew he was there because they saw a pair of bare, dark-brown, knobbly, long-toed, bony feet.

The feet came and stood right close by them. The feet emerged from beneath thin, white trousers, and as their eyes travelled all the way up, past a white tunic and brown waistcoat and past a red and blue woolly scarf around the neck, they found themselves looking into a round, shining, kind, wrinkly face, with deep-as-oceans large, brown eyes, and a mass of pure, white, fluffy hair which fell in a tangle over his brow.

From *Grandpa Chatterji* by Jamila Gavin

Thinking back

Write and say if each sentence is true (T) or false (F).

1 Sanjay and Neetu were brother and sister.
2 The children were waiting for their grandfather.
3 Their grandad arrived in a big shiny car.
4 The children hid under the table.
5 The children didn't hear Grandpa Chatterji come in.
6 Grandpa Chatterji was wearing a pair of soft slippers.

Thinking about it

1 Why were Neetu and Sanjay nervous?
2 Why do you think the children hid behind the sofa?
3 How can you tell the Grandpa Chatterji had come on a long journey?
4 Why do you think their grandad was not wearing shoes?
5 How do you know he had an old-looking face?
6 Do you think Grandpa was a friendly old man?

Thinking it through

1 Why do you think Sanjay and Neetu felt shy?
2 Have you ever felt shy when you have met someone for the first time? Who?
3 Write a description of Grandpa Chatterji.
4 How do you think Grandpa Chatterji will try and make friends with Sanjay and Neetu?